Natural, Permed, or Pressed

A Simple Guide to Growing Black Hair

By Shanet Dennis

Natural, Permed, or Pressed

A Simple Guide to Growing Black Hair

Copyright 2016 by Shanet Dennis

ISBN: 978-0-9977942-0-5

www.gabbrands.com

To every fly brother and sister out there who have inspired others to love the diversity of our hair by doing nothing more than allowing it to exist in all its glory!

Table of Contents

Introduction

T his little book is by no means and extensive text on the science of Black hair. This is not a book on how to go natural, or whose hair is better. This book was developed from one simple question—how did you grow your hair that long? I have answered this question hundreds of times, given out lists of what to do and how to do it, and held women's hands as they've gone through the process. For many years, I didn't realize this information was new to a lot of women. I assumed that people made informed choices about their hair and were happy with those choices. Today it is clear that this is not the case. So here we are—trying to find out the answer to the question of whether or not your hair can grow too. Well, the answer is ABSOLUTELY! But, you have to be willing to do the work. It is indeed, work!

When we think about how to grow hair the first thing that comes to mind is if our hair is actually growing from our scalps, and if so, why is it growing so slow? Our hair naturally grows at different rates, and in some areas or times of year it grows faster than others. This however, is not the meat and potatoes! What we really want to be talking about is hair *Retention.* What is happening to the hair once it has made its debut? The bottom line is this...once it gets here—you have to take care of it. As the hair grows you must keep in mind that the oldest part of your hair is the hair that has been around the longest—the ends. This is the hair that will require the most delicate care if it is going to be around for years to come. That being said, these are some general steps you can and should take for healthy growing hair!

Food

It's no secret that what we put inside of our bodies is reflected on the outside. Therefore, we truly are what we eat. Our hair and nails are the last parts of our bodies that receive nutrients, because these are the parts of our bodies that need them less. Therefore, if we are not eating foods with high nutritional value, these are the parts of the body that will suffer the most. Many people today are becoming more health conscientious, so this will be less of a concern for them (notice I said *them*). However, for those of us who live off of chips, cookies, candy, and cakes—we must think about the foods that may be contributing to our hair struggles. Some foods that have been known to be great for hair health include salmon, spinach, guava, sweet potatoes, cinnamon, eggs, and walnuts. Finally, drinking water is probably one the most important contributors to healthy hair, as the makeup of our entire bodies are 70 to 75 percent water. Not only will drinking plenty of water benefit the health our hair, but our skin will glow like the sun.

Supplements

There are a lot of great supplements on the market that are great for getting your hair growing. I grew up during a time where women were taking prenatal vitamins specifically to give their hair a growing boost. These days there are many healthy options without all of those additives that our body really don't need. One of the first natural products that I used religiously (because it actually works) was the Gueye Hair Growth Capsules. They are priced somewhere around $15 to $20 per bottle. You can get them at your local beauty supply or order online at www.gueye.com. This supplement is packed with good ingredients that benefit the hair, skin, and nails. When I took them (I kid you not) my hair was growing at a rate of 1 inch per month. The average hair growth rate is around ½ inch per month.

Another (more accessible) option is Biotin, which is a B complex vitamin that helps to increase the keratin structure of the hair. The FDA recommended dosage is about 200 mg, but I and many others take about 500 mg's for hair growth. You can purchase this at any local drug store or pharmacy. To really give your hair a kick start, you can try taking Biotin and MSM (Methyl-sulfonyl-methane) pills together. There is no recommended dosage for MSM, but the average dose for a super hair boost is 5000 mg. I would recommend a one month on and one month off approach to this combination for not more than six months.

Note: Be sure to drink 8 to 10 glasses of water per day while taking supplements.

Tools

L ow manipulation is key. Be gentle. Don't rake through the hair with combs and brushes. Our hair is fragile and daily combing and brushing does more harm than good. This is something that we rarely consider when thinking about hair care. Hard plastic bristle brushes are used to slick edges, ponytails, and slick backs. This constant raking rips our hair mid-strand, especially around the perimeter of the hair as this is the hair that is in first position to be attacked by our hair tools. This can be limited by purchasing quality soft boar bristle brushes, using the palm of your hand to do most of the work, and use the brush just for finishing touches. Fine tooth combs (especially the rat tale combs) are mostly used when the hair is straightened. These very fine teeth not only find tangles in the hair, but can create new ones. Using a wide tooth (seamless) comb is the better option for our strands. This comb rakes through the hair smoothly— allowing you to catch tangles with your fingers before accidently breaking the hair strands.

Bobby pins are great, but they don't last forever. Once the plastic head on the pin is split or removed—the bobby pin should be thrown out. Those split heads snag and rip the hair strands. Without that protective tip you could not only damage your hair, but your scalp as well. Rather than use rubber bands to secure ponytails or braids, try using Ouchless hair ties or satin covered scrunchies. Rubber bands do what? Say it with me…BREAK OUR HAIR!

Lastly, always sleep with a satin or silk scarf—NO MATTER WHAT. This applies even when your hair is not done. This protects your hair from breakage, and allows your hair to stay moisturized and manageable. Purchase a satin pillow case for the forgetful nights when you sleep with no scarf.

Washing

How often you wash your hair will vary based on styling preferences. For example, those who use a lot of hair products would need to wash more frequently than those who do not. On average, a healthy wash schedule is about every two weeks. The key to keeping your hair on your head during the washing process is to wash in sections. This could be 2, 4, 6, or 8—you choose. Gently massage the shampoo directly onto the scalp (not the length of the hair). Use palms of your fingertips only. Do not scratch with your fingernails as this will cause irritation or further exacerbate an existing scalp condition. Once you have thoroughly massaged your scalp, rinse the shampoo and allow the excess to clean the hair strands. It is not necessary to use additional product to wash the hair strands. Do this section by section and repeat if needed.

A healthy alternative to washing the hair with shampoo is the co-wash. This simply means washing your hair with conditioner or clarifying conditioner. The purpose is to gently cleanse the hair and scalp without stripping the hair of natural oils and needed hydration, especially for those who are natural. Simply follow the same steps as if you were washing with shampoo. Feel free to alternating between shampoo and co-washes based on your personal hair needs.

Note: Do not pile your hair on top of your head and vigorously scratch, scrub, and tug your hair clean. Doing this creates the perfect environment for matting, makes the detangling process so much more difficult, and results in preventable hair loss.

Conditioning

There is conditioning, and then there is deep conditioning. They are not one in the same. After your hair has been properly cleansed it is important to use conditioner to help restore nutrients lost during the wash, smooth the cuticle of the hair, and preserve moisture. Using the same sections created for washing, generously smooth conditioner in your hair avoiding the roots and scalp. Use the palms of your hands (praying hands) to distribute the product on the hair. You don't want to rake through with your fingers just yet. Give the product time to absorb and close the cuticle. Most directions on the bottle will tell you to leave it in for 1 to 2 minutes. I'd say, give it about 5 minutes and then begin detangling.

If you plan to use a significantly different product for deep conditioning, you can rinse thoroughly and then apply your deep conditioner using the praying hands method—being sure to maintain your sections. If you are layering product, you can skip the rinse. After applying your deep conditioner, cover with a plastic cap and sit under a hooded dryer for 20 to 30 minutes. If you prefer to avoid the heating process or do not own a dryer, you can use a plastic cap (or plastic grocery bag) and leave the conditioner in for a few hours. It is recommended that you deep condition once a week or at least twice a month if your hair is not in a long-term protective style.

Detangling

The best way to detangle the hair is by finger detangling, while wet, and with lots of conditioner. This means the primary (and sometimes the only) tools you will use are your fingers. After you have conditioned the hair, take 1 section and gently separate your hair a few strands at a time. When you feel your hair beginning to snag, simply spend a little extra time in that area to ensure you loosen any knots without breaking the hair strands. Once you have done this, you can gently comb through the section with your fingers. When you feel your hair is tangle free, you can (if you so choose) then use a wide tooth comb for one last attempt at getting rid of any tangles that your fingers may have missed. Be sure to start from the ends of the hair, working your way up to the roots. The end result is less hair on your shower walls or in your sink, and more on your head.

Sometimes it is necessary to detangle your hair when it is dry. For example, after taking down braids, weaves, or twists. Separating at the root and gently pulling the hairs apart before washing is an essential step to prevent matting and breakage. It may also be necessary to do a light finger detangle near the end of the day when the hair is in a straightened hair style.

Blow Drying

There are many styles that require the hair to be blown out. In such cases, you want to make sure you are doing this the safest way possible. I recommend using the tension method. Once the hair is rinsed and lightly air dried, take one section and pull taut. Without a blow-dryer comb or concentration nozzle, use sweeping motions up and down the hair shaft. Be sure to keep the dryer at least 6 inches away from the hair. Continue doing this until the section is dry and somewhat straight. Gently finger detangle and continue working with the section until you have achieved the desired result. You can opt to stop here.

For those who are looking for slightly straighter hair, you can opt to now use a wide tooth blow-dryer comb on the section. Be sure to start from the ends of the hair, working your way up to the roots. Continue this process on each section of hair. Once you are done, look around and notice how much less hair there is on the floor!

Heat Styling

This is one of the biggest issues related to the health and beauty of our hair. Some of us love our hair pressed, curled, sprayed and laid! While this look is just fine for those with naturally straight hair, most Black women have naturally kinky, coiled, and curly hair. Common knowledge tells us that things are in their optimum condition in their most natural form. This applies to our hair as well. So when we choose to alter it, we must handle it with great care. Heat damages our hair. There is no way around it. Our natural curls and coils slowly weaken, grow limp, and eventually break. With this knowledge, it should be made clear that every time we heat style we are taking a risk with our strands.

If you are a press and curl kind of girl, I would recommend only using extensive heat on the hair once a month. Many go to hair salons where they still utilize marcel irons, which is common practice in the Black hair community. Even working with these professionals, we still run the risk of scorching/burning our hair strands and wondering where that missing patch of hair went. To minimize this hair damage and hair loss, I would exclusively use **electric** flat irons or curling irons maybe once every two weeks maximum at a temperature of about 350 to 400 °F. The heat (though still damaging) is even and there is much less risk of unwanted damage.

Some people like to blow dry, press, pass the flat iron throughout the hair, and then curl with a curling iron or wand. Skipping the hot comb and choosing either the curling iron or flat iron is a better choice. A nice silky straight look can be achieved by blowing out the hair, taking small sections, and passing the flat iron across the hair once or twice. Many women in the natural hair community follow the one pass rule when it comes to flat ironing. When it comes to the curling iron or curling wand—the same rules apply. Though you are looking to achieve a curl, the hair is still being straightened through the heating process. So there is no need to use a flat iron prior to curling.

Ultimately, you should do what works best for you. Just know that every pass or additional heat on the strands can equal unwanted damage.

Natural Styling

Natural hair styling as defined here simply means without altering the natural texture of the hair and is the healthiest way to style our hair, but it is truly trial and error. There is no one fits all solution and not everything is going to work for everyone. However, it takes time to get to know what fits your life style and is a good representation of how you would like to present yourself to the world. There is so much versatility with natural styling that an entire book could be written on this topic alone. Since this little hand book is about hair growth and not just styling—I'll stick to the meat and potatoes! Wash n Go's, twists, braids, locks, weaves, twist outs, braid outs, afros, puffs, and buns, are all natural ways to style the hair. However, certain precautions should be taken with these styles as well.

Primarily, those who opt to wear *out* styles such as wash n go's, twist outs, braid outs, afros, and puffs must be mindful of tangles, drying, and single strand knots. Tangling is inevitable. Making sure you are using moisturizing products and staying consistent with a solid maintenance routine once or twice a week is imperative for hair retention. Those who wear protective styles such as twists, braids, weaves, and buns must still care for the hair even while it is being protected. This means moisturizing nightly with leave-in conditioners and oils, which will help maintain the hairs elasticity and significantly minimizes breakage. Protective styles are essential as they help to minimize daily manipulation of the hair, which is also a huge contributor to breakage.

Perms and Dyes

Many Black women love to change it up, while some just opt for simple convenience. This is what makes perms and dyes so popular. This may not apply to women who love to wear their hair short as they are able to work with a new head of hair every few months. But, for those of us who want to let it grow and let it flow—this is why you are here! Perms are very unhealthy for many reasons. First, they are permanent. Once you perm your hair that is it! The only way to go back to natural is to cut it off and start from scratch. Second, they weaken the hair cuticle, which can quickly cause breakage. Third, perms can cause irreversible damage to the scalp. These are just a few of the ways perms are not the best option for Black hair. But if you must use them, it is important to use them few and far between. Allow new hair to regenerate and give your scalp plenty of time to recover from the chemical process. This is called *stretching your relaxer*, which means allowing your new growth to sprout at least 1 or more inches before retouching.

Much of the information regarding perms applies when it comes to dyes. Though the visual results are different, the damage is essentially the same. Chemicals are chemicals; they all can cause great damage. When it comes to dyes, depositing color is not as harsh as lifting color from the hair. Be aware that bleaching can change the texture; causing the hair to become extremely dry and brittle, which means...breakage! If you can, I would recommend running in the opposite direction! But, if you must indulge in the beauty of the colored world—do away with do-it-yourself hair dyes and see a professional colorist.

Note: Not every professional stylist is a professional colorist. Do your research.

Edges

This was briefly mentioned in the Tools section, but deserves to be reiterated and expanded upon. The most fragile parts of Black hair are the ends and the edges. Because knowledge of how to properly care for our hair has waned in past years, many of us suffer from irreversible damage to our edges. The constant tugging and pulling from tight weaves, heavy braids, aggressive brushing, and pulling our hair into tight ponytails takes its toll. Without even realizing it—the hair eventually stops growing in those areas. This is called traction alopecia. If you have not suffered from this type of hair loss yet—you are in good shape. If you have, you can now be equipped with the information to save the hair you have left.

The hair around the perimeter of our head must be cared for in the gentlest ways possible. Be mindful of the materials on the inside of headbands, hats, and wigs. These materials rub against the hair or are secured tightly around the edges, which contributes to this type of hair loss. Look for satin or silk lined hair dresses and accessories. You can also add these materials yourself to the items you already own. In the meantime, be sure to wear a satin or silk scarf/bonnet underneath your wigs, hats, and beanies.

Remember, it takes a long time to grow your hair. Don't risk years' worth of growth for a *style of the day*!

Note: If you already have permanent damage there is a hair restoration doctor who specializes in African American hair types. His name is Dr. John Diep working out of the San Jose and San Francisco Bay Area.

Medical Hair Transplant & Aesthetics
1-866-999-6482
Hairdr@Mhtaclinic.Com

Trimming Split Ends

It seems like a paradox, but it is true. You must cut your hair in order to grow it. The good news is that you don't have to cut it every six weeks like many of us believed. Trimming the hair should be done as needed. If you are a person who subscribed to some of the unhealthy hair practices that were mentioned earlier, you might have to cut your hair more frequently. However, if you are properly caring for your hair, you will only have to cut it once or twice a year. With this understanding, there are a few things you should keep in mind. *If the split ends are not cut above where the hair begins to split, the hair will continue to spit up the hair shaft; damaging the healthy part of the hair strand.* Do not prolong cutting your hair if it is already split. Sometimes we hold on to this frazzled and lifeless hair for the sake of length. Doing this is defeating the purpose in theory and truth. Holding on to a few long strands of hair in a sea of broken ones is very unattractive, and intensify the existing damage over time. Find someone you trust to properly trim your hair or learn to do this yourself. There are hundreds of tutorials on YouTube that can show you how to do just that!

Products

Many products that are currently on the market will work just fine as long as they are used as directed. No person is the same and products work differently on different hair types. You must try different things to see what works best for you. Once you find those staple products, stick with them. However, it's important to keep in mind that if there is a primary ingredient in the product that you really like, you can get more of the benefit of that particular ingredient by going directly to the source. For all intents and purposes, here are some basic rules to follow. DO NOT USE ALCOHOL BASED STYLING GEL, POMADE GREASE, OR SUPER HOLDING SPRAYS ON YOUR HAIR. Pay attention to the ingredient list and avoid (as best you can) those that include petroleum, parabens, silicones, sulfates, mineral oils, and synthetic fragrances. These are either drying agents, clog the pores, or have other unknown ingredients. Gueye sells a fast grow oil that is good when you wear ponytails, weaves and braids. It contains a combination of some great organic ingredients and the cost is about $8. There are many natural oils that can be a benefit as well. My two favorites are organic coconut oil and organic grapeseed oil. Coconut oil can oxidize over time and leave an unpleasant odor. Grapeseed oil doesn't have a scent and is a light oil. Some other great oils are organic olive oil, jojoba oil, tea tree oil, castor oil, and organic raw shea butter. Find and use what works best for your hair.

Note: Gueye products can be found at www.gueye.com

Our Sons and Daughters

S ometimes our bad hair practices are passed down to our children. They watch what we do and want to imitate what *we believe* to be beautiful. It is important to teach our sons and daughters how to love, appreciate, and care for their hair. This starts by being the model. Weaves, wigs, and braid extensions are great protective styles and enhancers, but this means nothing if we are not in love with what is underneath. We want our sons to grow up with a preference of an image that is a reflection of themselves. Take these foundational tips and apply them to your children's hair. Teach them how to manage it while they are young, so that it does not feel like a hassle as they become older. Let's not again let a western European standard of beauty bury the beauty of our glorious Black hair, which we know is in an extraordinary class of its own.

Routine

Building a routine is probably the most vital component to ensuring that you remain consistent in your hair growth journey. You must plan your wash days. Plan when you are going to put your hair away by utilizing protective styles. Plan when you will wear your hair out, and when you will trim. Make the plan and stick to it. This will allow you to feel less frazzled when you have an event to attend, a bad hair day, or both! Know what your options are and keep them in the clutch for emergencies. My emergency hair style is the oversized faux bun using afro textured hair. This allows me to look chic in a manner of minutes with little to no effort. Use the following template to begin building a routine that can get you through a few months with little to no hassle. Then repeat!

- **Wash Day**- Products, tools, styling time
- **5 Day Style**- Products, tools, styling time
- **10 Day Style**- Products tools, styling time
- **30 Day Style**-Products tools, styling time
- **Go-to Style**-Products tools, styling time

Note: There will be times that you may have to deviate from your routine. For example, extended vacations and unexpected events may require a little tweaking of your original plans. Just remember that consistency is key.

My Personal Hair Routine

Wash once a month with Giovanni 50/50 balance clarifying shampoo. Co-wash once a week with Giovanni 50/50 balance hydrating calming conditioner. I deep condition once a week for a couple of hours under a plastic cap or grocery bag using organic coconut oil. I finger detangle in the shower, being careful not to rip through the hair. When I wear my hair curly, I don't rinse the conditioner out. I add grapeseed oil on top of it and twist my hair wet. Sometimes I pin the twists and wear them for the week, other times I wait for my hair to dry (overnight) and take the twists out. The twist-out is my go-to hairstyle! This style lasts for 6 days. I style my hair weekly unless it is in a straightened style.

I straighten my hair once every 3 to 4 months. I take the same previous steps, but I rinse all of the product out of my hair. I blow out the hair by pulling it taut with one hand and passing the warm air across the hair strands until they are dry (the tension method). I then gently blow dry the hair using a wide tooth blow dryer comb, and straighten with an electric flat iron no hotter than 375 F. I don't pass the flat iron across my hair more than twice. I also use the *chase method* when flat ironing. This style lasts 3 to 4 weeks without retouching or reapplying any type of heat.

If you have any further questions about styling options or anything else contact me on any of the following social media handles!

www.facebook.com/shanetdennisbooks
twitter.com/ShanetDennis
www.instagram.com/shanetdennis/

Also, take lots of pictures to document your progress. Especially for people who don't believe this will work!

Happy growing!

www.ingramcontent.com/pod-product-compliance
Lightning Source LLC
Chambersburg PA
CBHW071800020426
42331CB00008B/2345